Boldly Me

SELF-ESTEEM WORKBOOK

For Teen Girls

A Faith-Based Guide to Build your Confidence, Embrace Individuality and Step Into The Unique Masterpiece God Created You To Be

Hannelie Van Der Merwe

Boldly Me

Copyright © BeTheLight Publishing , 2024

All rights reserved. No portion of this book may be reproduced in any form without prior permission from the copyright owner of this book

Scripture Quatations are taken from THE HOLY BIBLE, NEW INTERNATIONAL VERSION®, NIV® Copyright © 1973, 1978, 1984, 2011 by Biblica, Inc.® Used by permission. All rights reserved worldwide.

These Scriptures are not shareware and may not be duplicated.

Limit of Liability/Disclaimer of warranty: The Publisher and the author make no representations of warranties with respect to the accuracy or completeness of the contents of this work and specifically disclaim all warranties, including without limitation warranties of fitness for a particular purpose. No warranty may be created or extended by sales or promotional materials. The advice and strategies contained herein may not be suitable for every situation. This work is sold with the understanding that the publisher is not engaged in rendering medical, legal, or other professional advice or services. If professional assistance is required, the services of a competent professional person should be sought. Neither the Publisher nor the author shall be liable for damages arising here from.

ISBN: Print Paperback 978-1-0686371-0-0

This Book Belongs To

_____

Date _____

Contents

Introduction	1
Getting Started	2
Part 1: KNOWING YOURSELF	4
Self-Love	5
Self Reflection	6
Unlock The Power Of Your Talents	11
Affirmations	17
Strengths & Achievements	24
How To Handle Challenges	30
Part 2: BUILDING CONFIDENCE	31
Body Positivity	32
Cultivate Self-Acceptance	37
Goal Settings	43
Celebrating Small Victories	52
Step Out Of Your Comfort Zone	56
Part 3: CULTIVATING SELF-WORTH	63
Self-Worth	64
Values	65
Mindfulness & Gratitude	73
Self-Care Routine	84
Part 4: EMBRACE INDIVIDUALITY	91
Understanding Uniqueness	92
Own Your Uniqueness	93
Show Your Uniqueness	95
Embrace Individuality	103
Part 5: SOCIAL CONNECTIONS	107
Relationships	108
Setting Friendship Boundaries	111
Conclusion	118
Puzzle Solutions	120

Boldly Me

INTRODUCTION

Dear Bold and Beautiful You,

Welcome to a journey of self-discovery, empowerment, and unapologetic self-love. This workbook, "Boldly Me," is crafted with you in mind.

In these pages, we're going to explore together, aiming to boost your confidence, strengthen your sense of worth, and help you embrace the unique masterpiece God created in you.

Adolescence is a time of growth, both physically and emotionally, and it's our belief that by understanding and embracing yourself, you can navigate this journey with resilience, authenticity, and joy.

This workbook is more than just sheets to fill in—it's a space for you to discover the power within yourself, the incredible love that God has for you, and the beautiful person He made you to be. Each exercise, activity, and reflection is a step towards understanding your unique qualities, achievements, and the limitless potential God has placed within you.

Always remember that you are not alone in this journey. God walks beside you, guiding each step, and within these pages, you'll find tools to build a foundation of confidence, embrace your individuality, and cultivate a deep appreciation for the extraordinary person God created you to be.

So, let's start the journey, explore the depths of your incredible spirit, and boldly declare, "I am fearfully and wonderfully made" (Psalm 139:14). Your journey to self-love begins now.

Lots of Love

Boldly Me

As you start this exciting self-love adventure, take a moment to think about what you hope to learn and achieve from this book.

Intentions are like the compass guiding your ship through unexplored waters. It is very much like goals. They give you direction, purpose, and focus. By setting intentions, you declare to yourself that this journey matters, that you matter, and that the steps you're about to take are purposeful and meaningful.

Now, there are different ways to set intentions.

What do you hope to achieve by the end of this journey? What are your goals? Is it more confidence, a deeper understanding of yourself, or a greater sense of self-worth?

Take a moment to think about your goals and write them down.

....
....
....
....
....
....

Getting Started

> Imagine yourself at the end of this workbook—feeling confident, sure of yourself, and loving everything that makes you unique.

2 Visualize Success

Picture in your mind all the positive changes you want to see in your life.

....
....
....

3 Empowering Words

> Think of words that show the positive changes you wish to experience.
>
> Choose words that resonate with you.

Circle your positive empowering words.

Brave	Confident	Helpful	Curious
Strong	Happy	Caring	Resilient
Kind	Joyful	Loving	Honest
Smart	Determined	Unique	Respectful
Creative	Courageous	Adventurous	Grateful

Part 1

KNOWING YOURSELF

Knowing Yourself

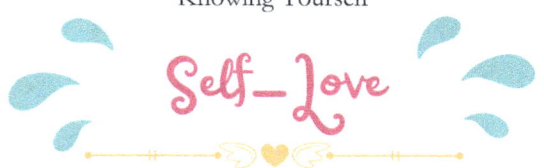

Did you know you have the incredible power to shape your life story and define the path ahead? But to do that, we must take the time to get to know ourselves. Knowing yourself is about understanding your strengths, quirks, dreams, and fears and "Boldly Me" is your special tool, helper, and safe place to discover more about yourself. But first things first...

Let's talk about
SELF-LOVE

Self-love is a powerful and positive concept that involves treating yourself with kindness, acceptance, and care. It means appreciating and valuing who you are, just as you are, and recognizing your own worth.

Imagine you have a close friend whom you care about deeply. You support and encourage them, celebrate their successes, and understand and forgive when they make mistakes. Self-love is about extending that same level of compassion and kindness to yourself. It's about being your own best friend and treating yourself with the same love and respect you would offer to someone you care about.

Remember, self-love is a journey, not a destination. It's something you can develop over time by being patient and gentle with yourself. It's about realizing that you are deserving of love and treating yourself with the same kindness and compassion that you offer to others.

... be you
... do you
... love you
... for you

Boldly Me

Self-Reflection

Imagine you have a personal gallery showcasing your unique talents and creations. What would be on display?

....
....
....
....

Think about the things you do that make you happy, especially the fun and creative activities you enjoy! It could be a hobby, a craft, or any activity that allows you to express yourself in a unique and joyful way.

List three specific creative activities or hobbies that bring you joy and make you feel happy.

....
....
....
....

Hobbies are whispers of self-care to the soul, speaking volumes of joy, relaxation, and mental harmony in the language of passion.

Knowing Yourself

Think about a problem in the world that really matters to you. It could be about helping people, caring for animals, or protecting nature.

What change would you like to see, and how can you help make it happen?

....
....
....
....
....
....
....
....

Values shape character; Character shapes destiny

Values are the important beliefs and ideas that you carry in your heart and that you stand by in difficult times, helping you know what is right or wrong. (for examples Kindness, honesty, respect, responsibility, courage, fairness etc.)

Write down three values that are really important to you.

....
....
....
....
....
....

Boldly Me

Think of books, music, or movies that really grab your attention.

Why do you enjoy them so much? Do you notice any special ideas or stories in them that you really connect with?

....
....
....
....
....
....

List your three favorite books, songs, and movies, and identify the values or interests that speak to you.

My favorite MOVIES

....
....
....

My favorite SONGS

....
....
....

Identify all the types of genres that you like to read.

My favorite BOOKS

....
....
....

I like to read ...

- ☐ Fiction
- ☐ Non-Fiction
- ☐ Mystery
- ☐ Thriller
- ☐ Romance
- ☐ Science Fiction (Sci-Fi)
- ☐ Fantasy
- ☐ Historical Fiction
- ☐ Horror
- ☐ Adventure
- ☐ Biography
- ☐ Self-Help
- ☐ Philosophy
- ☐ Poetry
- ☐ Comedy
- ☐ Drama
- ☐ Crime
- ☐ Young Adult (YA)
- ☐ Science
- ☐ Travel
- ☐ Cookbooks
- ☐ Autobiography

Knowing Yourself

Imagine you have a magic bracelet, and each charm tells a story about who you are. What special symbols or pictures would you choose to show what makes you unique? If someone looked at your bracelet, they'd instantly understand what kind of person you are.

Draw your charms below and explain why they are important to you.

"I praise you because I am fearfully and wonderfully made; your works are wonderful, I know that full well."
— Psalm 139:14 (NIV)

Boldly Me

Imagine what you want to be when you grow up, achieving your dreams and being really happy.

What ACTIVITIES, CAREERS, or ADVENTURES do you see yourself doing in the future?

What do you look for in a friend? What makes a good friend to you? Write a list of qualities you think are important in a friend, and then choose one quality and write a short explanation of why you think it is important.

Knowing Yourself

Unlock the Power of Your Talents

The Parable of the Bags of Gold
Read Matthew 25:14-30 (NIV)

Lets talk about the story

Imagine being entrusted with a bag of gold. In the bible story Jesus shared, each servant received a different amount based on their ability. Now, this isn't just about literal gold coins—it's a powerful metaphor for the unique gifts, skills, and potential that God has given each one of us.

Understanding the Metaphor

In the Bible, a "talent" isn't just a skill; it's your unique set of abilities, gifts, and even your personality. God has gifted each one of us in different ways, tailoring these gifts to who we are. Just like the servants in the story, you have been given a specific amount of "gold" based on your unique abilities and potential.

Multiplying Your Talents

The moral of the story is clear: God wants us to use and multiply the gifts He has given us. Just like the servants who invested and gained more, God desires us to explore, nurture, and share our talents. It's not about comparison or competition; it's about embracing and growing the unique gifts that make you who you are.

Taking Initiative

The master praised the servants who took initiative, worked with what they had, and multiplied their talents. Similarly, God delights in seeing you step into your abilities, explore new skills, and make a positive impact. It's not about having the most talents but what you do with what you have.

Overcoming Fear and Doubt

In the story, one servant buried his talent out of fear. God doesn't want us to hide or be afraid of using our gifts. Your unique qualities are meant to shine, not to be hidden away. Don't let fear or self-doubt bury the incredible potential within you.

Embracing Growth and Responsibility

God sees your efforts, no matter the scale. Whether it's a small or significant step, each effort counts. Just like the master rewarded the faithful servants with more responsibility, God promises that as you use your talents, He'll entrust you with even greater opportunities and blessings.

Conclusion

The bags of gold symbolize your talents. It's not about comparison but about embracing your unique gifts, taking initiative, overcoming fear, and using your abilities to make a positive impact. Remember, your talents are a divine investment, and the journey of discovering and multiplying them is a beautiful part of your unique story.

Knowing Yourself

What are your unique talents and skills that make you stand out?

....
....
....
....
....
....

How do you feel when you share your special skills and show what you're good at?

....
....
....
....
....
....

Can you identify moments in your life when you felt truly confident and happy performing or showing off your skills? Write them down below.

....
....
....
....
....

Boldly Me

Who or what inspires you to keep pushing forward, even when faced with difficulties?

....
....
....

> *Your talents are the unique brushstrokes that paint the masterpiece of your purpose.*

What short-term and long-term goals do you have for developing and showcasing your talents?

....
....
....
....
....
....
....
....

Do you think practice is important for developing talents? Why or why not?

....
....
....
....
....
....
....

Knowing Yourself

What activities make you lose track of time because you enjoy them so much?

....
....
....
....
....

Have you ever tried something new and found out you were really good at it? How did that make you feel?

....
....
....
....
....
....
....

What's something you've always wanted to try but haven't yet? How do you think you could start developing that talent?

....
....
....
....
....
....
....

Boldly Me

How do you think your talents could help you in the future?

Do you think it's important to keep trying even when you face challenges while developing your talents? Why or why not?

> "Whatever you do, work at it with all your heart, as working for the Lord, not for human masters, since you know that you will receive an inheritance from the Lord as a reward. It is the Lord Christ you are serving."
> – Colossians 3:23-24 (NIV)

Knowing Yourself

Affirmations

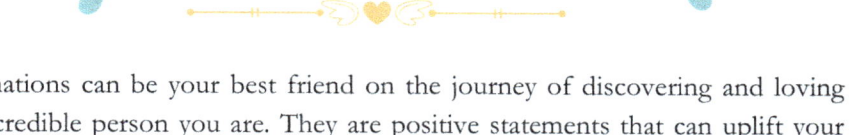

Affirmations can be your best friend on the journey of discovering and loving the incredible person you are. They are positive statements that can uplift your spirits, boost your confidence, and develop a mindset of self-love.

Let's look at the world of affirmations and learn how to write effective affirmations.

1. Start with Positivity

Affirmations are all about positive vibes. Begin your affirmations with empowering and uplifting words. **For example, instead of saying**

"I am not afraid," say
"I am brave and courageous."

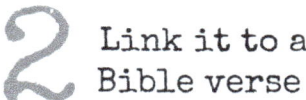

2. Link it to a Bible verse

The Bible is filled with positive and uplifting messages. Linking affirmations to Bible verses reinforces these positive messages, providing a solid foundation for building a mindset of optimism, gratitude, and confidence.

> "For God gave us a spirit not of fear but of power and love and self-control." – 2 Timothy 1:7

3 Be Present

Frame your affirmations in the present tense, as if they are already true. This helps your mind align with the positive vision you're creating.

Instead of saying

"I will be confident."

say

"I am confident."

4 Personalize it

Make your affirmations uniquely yours. Tailor them to reflect your goals, values, and desires. The more personal and meaningful they are, the more impact they'll have.

Remember, affirmations are like seeds of positivity that you plant in your mind. With time, care, and belief, these seeds can blossom into a garden of self-love and confidence.

You are worthy of all the positive affirmations you speak into your life.

"I can do all things through Him who strengthens me." - Philippians 4:13

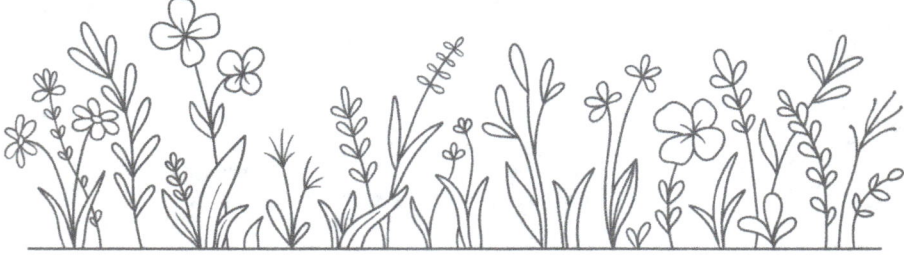

Knowing Yourself

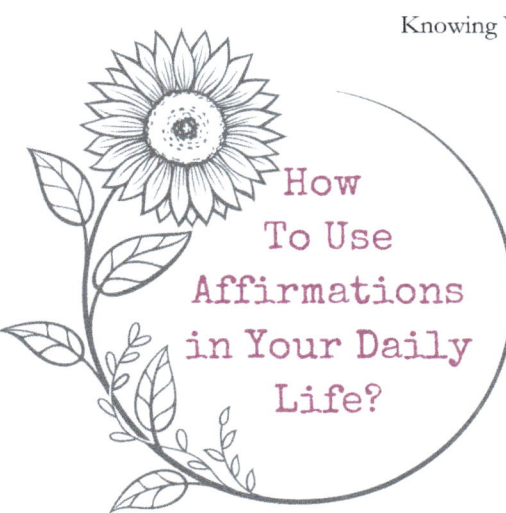

How To Use Affirmations in Your Daily Life?

1. Morning Routine

Include affirmations into your morning routine. Stand in front of the mirror, look yourself in the eyes, and say your affirmations out loud. Believe in the words you speak.

2. Write Them Down

Write down your affirmations in a special notebook or sticky notes. The act of writing reinforces the positive messages and makes them more tangible.

3. Use Sticky Notes

Place sticky notes with affirmations on your mirror, desk, or anywhere you'll see them frequently. Let these positive reminders brighten your day.

4. Visualization

As you repeat your affirmations, visualize the positive outcomes. Imagine yourself acting/living the qualities and achievements mentioned in your affirmations.

Use Color ...

when writing down your affirmations or use different color sticky notes.

Affirmations and Bible Verses

I am fearfully and wonderfully made.

Psalm 139:14 - "I praise you because I am fearfully and wonderfully made; your works are wonderful, I know that full well."

I am strong and courageous.

Joshua 1:9 - "Have I not commanded you? Be strong and courageous. Do not be afraid; do not be discouraged, for the Lord your God will be with you wherever you go."

I am loved unconditionally.

Romans 8:38-39 - "For I am convinced that neither death nor life, neither angels nor demons, neither the present nor the future, nor any powers, neither height nor depth, nor anything else in all creation, will be able to separate us from the love of God that is in Christ Jesus our Lord."

I am a light in the world.

Matthew 5:14 - "You are the light of the world. A town built on a hill cannot be hidden."

I am chosen and set apart.

1 Peter 2:9 - "But you are a chosen people, a royal priesthood, a holy nation, God's special possession, that you may declare the praises of Him who called you out of darkness into His wonderful light."

I am created for a purpose.

Jeremiah 29:11 - "For I know the plans I have for you, declares the Lord, plans for welfare and not for evil, to give you a future and a hope."

I am clothed in strength and dignity.

Proverbs 31:25 - "She is clothed with strength and dignity; she can laugh at the days to come."

Knowing Yourself

In this space, create your own personalized affirmations. Next, cut them out and put them where you'll see them every day.

Boldly Me

Knowing Yourself

Fill in the open spaces with your own affirmations inspired by the Bible! Let them guide and uplift you each day.

I trust in God's plan for my life, and I know He has great things in store for me.

I am fearfully and wonderfully made in the image of God.

I find strength in God's Word, and it guides me in all aspects of my life.

I can do all things through Christ who strengthens me.

I walk in faith, not in fear, for God is with me always.

Strengths & Achievements

List three strengths or qualities that you are really good at or proud of about yourself.

....
....
....

> Your strength is not in fitting in, but in standing out.

What are some compliments you often receive from friends, family, or teachers?

....
....
....
....
....
....

Ask a friend or family member: "What do you think are my greatest strengths?"

....
....
....
....
....
....

Knowing Yourself

Think about a challenging situation. How can you change your perspective to see it as a chance to use your strengths and bounce back?

....
....
....
....
....
....

Think about times when things changed, and you adapted well. How did you handle it? Please be sure to include the strength you showed in adjusting to different situations.

> "To improve is to change; to be perfect is to change often."
>
> Winston Churchill

Boldly Me

Reflect on areas where you've grown personally. It could be facing fears, improving discipline, or gaining new perspectives. Acknowledge the strengths that helped you grow.

....

....

....

....

....

....

....

....

Find words related to personal strength

Puzzle 1

Resilient
Tenacious
Capable
Empathetic
Empowered
Fearless
Inspirational
Confident
Determined
Courageous

Z	B	S	X	F	X	I	Z	K	E	B	V	C	C	H	J	Z	C
T	R	R	T	V	X	Q	D	I	F	M	Q	Q	C	Y	Q	A	K
Q	E	M	P	A	T	H	E	T	I	C	G	H	Z	J	X	B	Z
N	S	Z	I	P	W	X	T	H	W	P	G	R	S	L	U	O	A
U	I	F	E	A	R	L	E	S	S	J	T	A	X	Y	Q	N	C
X	L	I	N	S	P	I	R	A	T	I	O	N	A	L	R	U	O
K	I	U	H	M	T	E	M	P	O	W	E	R	E	D	C	D	N
Q	E	Z	X	V	O	K	I	T	U	S	X	C	F	Y	N	Y	F
S	N	U	S	Y	F	R	N	I	U	V	H	T	C	K	J	W	I
V	T	U	D	Y	D	M	E	I	A	H	V	E	D	Y	B	A	D
L	F	P	C	G	O	I	D	I	A	J	F	N	A	W	X	A	E
J	F	X	C	A	P	A	B	L	E	X	A	A	R	G	P	U	N
T	G	N	P	P	O	K	C	Z	P	V	A	C	T	L	Z	B	T
V	L	G	I	D	Q	Z	Q	D	L	E	M	I	M	Q	N	X	H
L	F	O	Q	H	H	N	Y	S	O	U	U	O	I	J	H	A	V
Y	Z	C	J	Z	F	D	Z	K	X	A	F	U	E	S	V	P	H
D	K	X	C	O	U	R	A	G	E	O	U	S	S	C	C	L	M
U	B	B	C	G	A	O	K	Q	F	J	U	D	M	D	C	T	O

Knowing Yourself

List all your achievements, both big and small. Write down the details of each accomplishment and reflect on how it made you feel.

> I am a one-of-a-kind creation, and my uniqueness is my greatest strength.

Boldly Me

Think back on times when you made a difference in someone else's life. It could be by being kind or lending a hand. Reflect on how your actions were meaningful and changed things for the better.

Share a moment when you felt you made a mistake or faced a challenge. How did you handle it, and what did you learn from the experience?

Remember, everyone makes mistakes, and they can be valuable lessons.

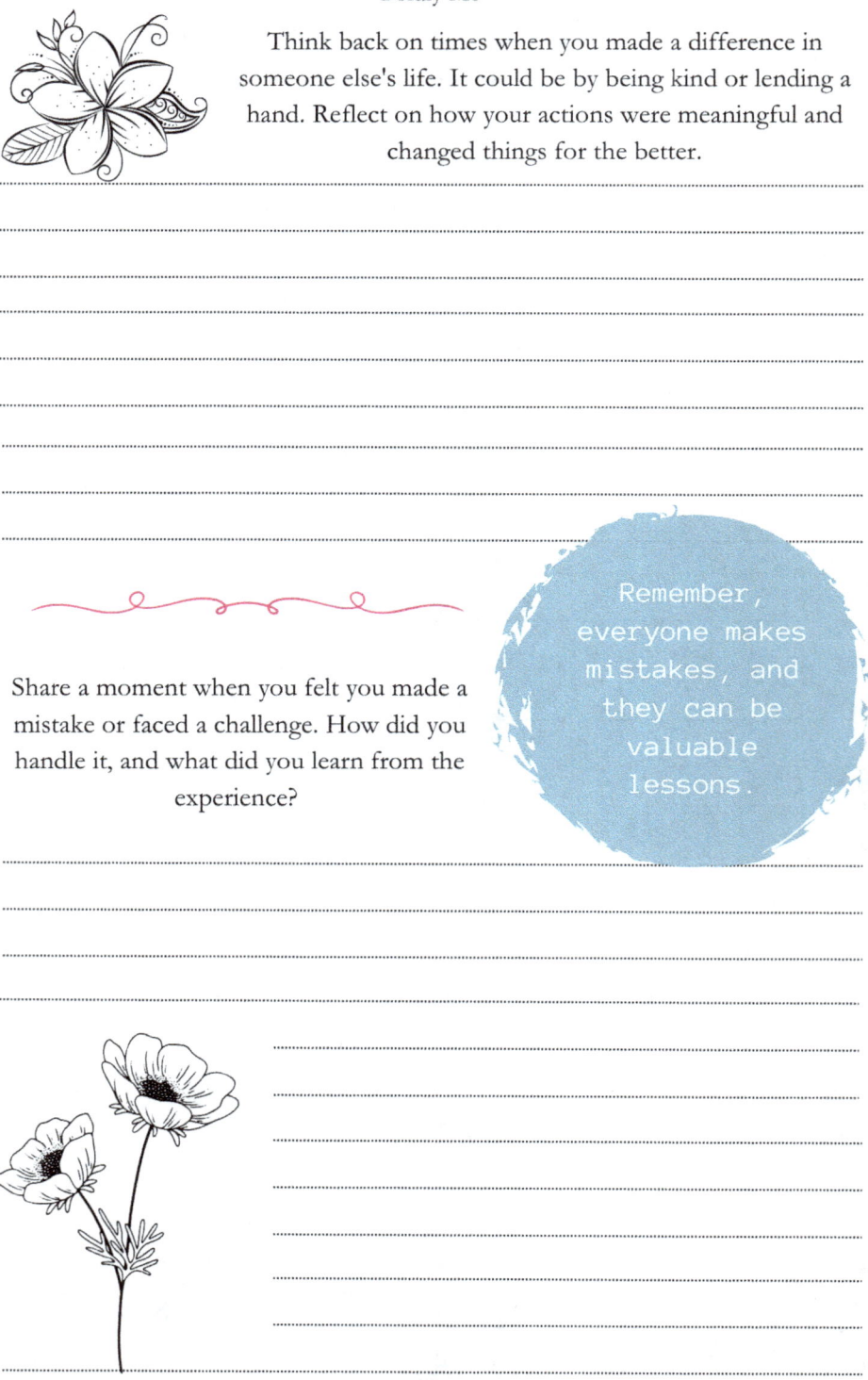

Knowing Yourself

In what ways can you show kindness to yourself during challenging times?

....
....
....
....
....
....

> Instead of being overly critical, talk to yourself with the same kindness you would offer to a friend facing a similar challenge.

> Dedicate time to activities that bring you joy and relaxation. Whether it's reading, listening to music, or engaging in a hobby, prioritize what makes you happy.

ow to Handle Challenges

Life is like a wild adventure, full of ups and downs, victories, and tough times. When we face challenges, that's when we really see how strong we are. Challenges might seem scary, but they're chances for us to grow and show how tough we can be.

When things get tough, remember that every problem is like a step toward success. It's not about avoiding challenges but having the courage to face and beat them. Think of each difficulty as an opportunity to improve yourself, build endurance, and show your inner strength.

To conquer challenges, it's important to have a POSITIVE mindset. Instead of worrying about what might go wrong, focus on what you can learn and achieve. Challenges aren't roadblocks; they're paths guiding you to become a better and more self-aware person.

Surround yourself with people who encourage and support you. Share your challenges because being open about them is a sign of strength. Ask for advice, help others, and get inspiration from those who've faced similar obstacles. You're not alone on this journey.

Break big challenges into smaller, doable steps. Celebrate every little win and recognize your progress. Setbacks aren't failures; they're chances to learn, adjust, and try again.

Most importantly, believe in your ability to bounce back. Challenges aren't here to break you but to make you stronger, wiser, and more caring. Your strength in overcoming challenges shows your inner power. Embrace the journey, face challenges with determination, and let each obstacle push you toward success.

Part 2

Building Confidence

Boldly Me

Body Positivity

Make a list of at least ten things you appreciate about your body. These can include physical features, abilities, or even the way your body allows you to engage with the world.

....
....
....
....
....
....
....
....
....
....
....
....

List three qualities that make you beautiful beyond just how you look.

....
....
....
....
....

Building Confidence

Sit in front of a mirror and write down your thoughts and feelings as you look at yourself. Challenge negative thoughts and focus on positive aspects.

Write a LOVE note to yourself on the mirror.

....
....
....
....
....

Look directly into your eyes in the mirror and say these words out loud.

"I am grateful for my unique and wonderful body. Every curve, every mark, and every part is a testament to my individuality and strength.
I choose to honor and love my body, recognizing it as the beautiful and capable creation it is. I accept my uniqueness, and with gratitude, I create a positive and loving relationship with my body every day."

I praise you because I am fearfully and wonderfully made; your works are wonderful, I know that full well. – Psalm 139:14 (NIV)

Boldly Me

Write a letter to your body, thanking it for everything it does for you. Focus on the parts you love and appreciate. Acknowledge its strength and resilience and how it lets you live life to the fullest.

Building Confidence

Create a list of positive affirmations specifically related to your body. Use empowering words to affirm your body's uniqueness, strength, and beauty. Repeat these affirmations daily.

Boldly Me

Building Confidence

Cultivate Self-Acceptance

First things first: You are incredible just as you are!

Your quirks, strengths, and uniqueness make you who you are, and that's something truly special. It's easy to look at others and wish you had something they do, but remember, they're probably looking at you and thinking the same thing.

Your body is your ally, not your enemy

It's not about fitting into a specific mold; it's about feeling strong, healthy, and comfortable.
Nourish your body with love and care because it's the only one you've got, and it's pretty amazing.

Set boundaries

It's okay to say no to things that don't align with your values or make you uncomfortable. Prioritize your well-being and surround yourself with people who lift you up.

Mistakes happen.

They are not a reflection of your worth or intelligence but opportunities to learn and grow. Be kind to yourself, just like you would to a friend who made a mistake. You're exploring new things, and it's fine if you don't know everything yet.

Celebrate your victories, big and small

Acknowledge your achievements, whether it's doing really well in a test, overcoming a fear, or simply getting through a tough day. You deserve it!

Remember, you're a work in progress, and that's perfectly okay

Life is a journey of self-discovery, and you're constantly changing. Welcome the changes, celebrate the wins, and most importantly, be kind to yourself along the way.

You're not alone in this journey.

Reach out to friends, family, or someone you trust when you need support. And always, always be your own biggest cheerleader. Because, my dear, you are worth it.

Building Confidence

Think back to a moment when you felt truly comfortable in your own skin. What were you doing, and how can you recreate that feeling more often?

....
....
....
....
....
....

List three things you appreciate about yourself, both inside and out. How do these unique qualities shape who you are as a person?

....
....
....
....
....
....

Create a collection of compliments from friends, family, or even yourself. When feeling self-doubt, revisit this collection for a confidence boost.

you are wonderful

Boldly Me

Describe three activities that make you feel loved and cared for. How can you incorporate these into your routine for improved self-acceptance?

"I deserve moments of self-care, and by honoring myself, I cultivate a resilient and vibrant existence."

Building Confidence

What role do you think social media plays in influencing our self-perception, and how can we use it positively?

....
....
....
....
....
....
....
....
....

Role Models

Identify three women you admire for their strength and authenticity. What qualities do they have that you would like to adopt in yourself?

....
....
....
....
....
....

Boldly Me

What advice would you give to someone struggling to accept themselves, especially when faced with societal pressures and comparisons to others? How can they develop self-compassion and focus on their unique strengths and qualities?

....
....
....
....
....
....
....
....
....
....
....
....

Create a playlist of songs that uplift and empower you, focusing on messages that promote body positivity and self-acceptance. Use the space below to begin listing the songs you know.

Building Confidence

Goal Setting

Let's talk about something that can truly transform your life: **Goal Setting**. It might sound like a grown-up thing, but trust me, it's a game-changer for your personal achievements and growth.

Guiding Your Journey

Setting goals is like having a roadmap for your dreams. Imagine going on an epic adventure without any idea where you're heading – goals give you direction, purpose, and a clear path to follow.

Empowering Your Dreams

Goals turn your dreams into achievable targets. Whether it's acing that tough exam, learning a new skill, or chasing your passions, setting goals empowers you to turn your visions into reality.

Building Confidence

Achieving even small goals boosts your confidence. It's like scoring a victory, reminding you of your capabilities. With every goal conquered, you become more resilient and ready to face new challenges.

Focus and Prioritization

In a world buzzing with distractions, goals help you stay focused. They guide you on what truly matters to you, making it easier to prioritize and invest your time and energy wisely.

Learning and Growing

Goals are your personal teachers. They push you out of your comfort zone, helping you discover strengths and talents you never knew existed. Every setback is a chance to learn and grow, even if you stumble.

Shaping Your Future

Your goals are the architects of your future. By setting clear intentions today, you're actively shaping the life you want to lead tomorrow. It's like being the author of your own story.

Don't be afraid to **DREAM BIG** and set those goals. Whether big or small, GOALS are the stepping stones to the incredible person you're becoming. Embrace the journey, celebrate your victories, and let your goals be the guiding stars lighting up your path to success!

Building Confidence

Ways To Help You Set Your

GOALS

1. Vision Board Creation

Collect magazines, images, and words that connect with your dreams and ambitions. Arrange these on a board or paper to craft a vision board. This visual representation will inspire you daily to achieve your goals and aspirations.

2. Break down your goals using the SMART method

1. **Specific**: Make your goal clear and specific, so you know exactly what you want to achieve.
2. **Measurable**: Ensure your goal is measurable, so you can track your progress and know when you've reached it.
3. **Achievable**: Set goals that are realistic and possible for you to reach with your current resources and abilities.
4. **Relevant**: Make sure your goal aligns with your interests, values, and long-term goals.
5. **Time-bound**: Set a realistic deadline for your goal to create a sense of urgency and motivate action.

3. Goal Reflection Journal

Dedicate a journal to your goals. Regularly reflect on your progress, setbacks, and the lessons learned. Use this space to adjust your strategies and celebrate small victories along the way.

4 Mind Mapping

Create a mind map centered around your main goal. Branch out with sub-goals, actions, and potential challenges. This visual representation helps you see the interconnected elements of your goal and plan accordingly.

5 Goal Pyramid

Visualize your goal as the peak of a pyramid. Break it down into smaller, manageable steps that form the foundation. With each step you complete, you climb closer to your ultimate goal. This method offers a structured way to achieve bigger dreams.

Remember, goal setting is a flexible process, and it's okay to adjust your goals as circumstances change. Regularly revisit and reassess your goals to make sure they align with your changing priorities and aspirations.

Building Confidence

Let's Get Started On Your GOALS

Identify Your Goal

Start by clearly defining what you want to achieve. Make sure your goal is Specific, Measurable, Achievable, Relevant, and Time-bound. This will help you create a clear plan for achieving it.

Break it Down + Set Deadlines

Break down your goal into smaller, manageable steps to make it easier to track your progress and stay motivated. Set deadlines for each step to create a sense of urgency and keep yourself focused on completing tasks on time.

Steps	Deadlines

Create a Plan

Develop a detailed plan outlining how you will achieve each step of your goal. Consider what resources you'll need and how you'll overcome any obstacles.

_____
_____
_____
_____
_____
_____
_____
_____
_____
_____
_____
_____
_____
_____
_____
_____

Stay Flexible

Be open to adjusting your plan as needed. Life can be unpredictable, so it's important to remain flexible and adapt to changes along the way.

Stay Accountable

Share your goal with others and ask for their support. Having someone to hold you accountable can help keep you motivated and on track.

Boldly Me

Use this space to plan your goal using the Mind Map technique.

Building Confidence
Track Your Progress

Regularly monitor your progress towards your goal. Celebrate your successes and adjust your plan if necessary to keep moving forward.

Write down your goals for each step and define what success looks like for each goal. Ask, "How will I know when I've achieved this goal?" . Set clear and measurable criteria to track your progress and celebrate your achievements as you reach each milestone.

My Goals	Success when ...

Building Confidence

Stay Positive

Maintain a positive mindset throughout your goal-setting journey. Focus on your strengths and remember that setbacks are a natural part of the process.

Reminder of my strengths

Celebrate Your Success

Once you've achieved your goal, take time to celebrate your success and acknowledge your hard work. Then, set new goals and continue striving for personal growth and development.

Philippians 4:13 - "I can do all things through Christ who strengthens me."

Boldly Me

The Magic of Celebrating Small Victories

On life's journey, it's easy to focus on the grand milestones, the big wins that everyone notices. But it turns out that celebrating these tiny triumphs is like a secret weapon, fueling your journey in the most magical way.

Light Your Spark

Celebrating small victories is like adding sparkles to your motivation. Each little win reminds you of your capabilities, light that inner fire and keeping it shining bright.

Building Positivity

When you celebrate the small stuff, it's like turning up the volume on positivity. It helps you shift your focus from what's not done to what you've achieved. Positive vibes all the way!

Growing Your Confidence

Confidence isn't just about big achievements; it grows with every small victory. Each win adds a brick to your confidence wall, making you believe in yourself a little more each time.

Building Momentum

Small victories are like a secret medicine for momentum. They break down big goals into doable steps, helping you keep that progress train chugging along.

Building Confidence

Recognizing Your Growth

You're on a journey of growth, and those small victories are your signposts. Celebrating them helps you see how far you've come and appreciate the journey you're on.

Discovering Your Superpowers

Celebrating small victories is like unlocking superpowers. It prompts you to reflect on your efforts and learn valuable lessons. You're basically a superhero in the making!

Turning Your Journey into an Adventure

Life's an adventure, and celebrating small victories turns it into a joy ride. It helps you find joy in the little things, making the journey itself something to celebrate.

Bouncing Back Stronger

Life can throw curveballs, but small victories act like superhero shields, making you bounce back stronger. They teach you to handle challenges with style and resilience.

Feeling the Gratitude Vibes

Small victories teach you to be grateful for the journey. They make you appreciate the progress, the friends who cheer you on, and all the cool opportunities that come your way.

So, remember to give yourself a high-five for those small victories. Whether it's finish reading a book, overcoming a tough day, or just being awesome, take a moment to celebrate. They're like the glitter on the cupcakes of life – making it sweeter and more fun!

Boldly Me

Celebrating victories doesn't always have to involve a big party. Here are 10 creative and meaningful ways for you to celebrate your achievements:

Spa Day at Home

Treat yourself to a spa day at home. Take a long bath, use skincare products, and pamper yourself with relaxation.

Solo Movie Night

Enjoy a solo movie night with your favorite films, snacks, and a cozy blanket. It's a perfect way to unwind and celebrate on your own terms.

Bookstore or Online Book Shopping

If you love reading, visit a bookstore or indulge in some online book shopping. Treat yourself to a new book as a reward.

Artistic Expression

Engage in artistic expression. Whether it's painting, drawing, or writing, use a creative way to celebrate your achievements.

Fitness Adventure

Try a new fitness class or activity that you've been curious about. It's a great way to celebrate your physical and mental well-being.

Shopping Spree

Treat yourself to a shopping spree. Whether it's a new outfit, accessories, or something you've had your eye on, pick out items that make you feel fantastic.

Building Confidence

Personalized Gifts

Consider buying yourself a personalized gift that holds sentimental value. It could be a piece of jewellery, a custom item, or something that reflects your personality.

Create a Celebration Playlist

Curate a playlist of songs that resonate with your achievements. Listen to it while enjoying your treats or during your shopping spree.

Capture the Moment

Take photos to commemorate your celebration. Document the items you purchased or the moments spent savoring your favorite treats.

Share the Joy

If you're comfortable, share your celebration on social media. It's a way to spread positivity and inspire others with your accomplishments.

Add to the list thinking of ways you would like to celebrate your goals.

....
....
....
....
....
....
....
....
....
....
....

Boldly Me

Time To Step Out Of Your Comfort Zone

Let's talk about the superhero power you have within ...

COURAGE

Courageous acts are like your superhero cape, allowing you to face challenges, be true to yourself, and embrace the incredible person you are becoming. It's not about being fearless; it's about doing what scares you, standing tall in the face of uncertainty, and realizing your own strength.

Imagine sharing your thoughts even when they might be different from others or trying new things that spark your interest.

Courage is found in moments like these—when you set healthy boundaries, prioritize your well-being, and stand up for your dreams. It's about admitting when you make mistakes, learning from them, and growing stronger.

Courage means following your passions fearlessly and embracing what makes you unique. Each time you face a challenge, no matter how small, you're adding to your story of bravery, filled with empowerment, resilience, and the unstoppable spirit of a true heroine.

So, wear your courage like a crown, and let it guide you through the exciting journey of discovering the superhero within.

Building Confidence
Practical Ways To Be Bold and Courages

After completing one of these courageous acts, check the box below the prompt. Once you've checked all five boxes, take a moment to celebrate your accomplishments!

Join a New Club or Activity

Explore interests beyond your usual routine by joining a club or activity you've never tried. Whether it's a sports team, art class, or debate club, engaging in new experiences introduces you to different people and perspectives.

Public Speaking Challenge

Face the fear of public speaking by volunteering to give a short presentation at school or joining a public speaking club. This helps build confidence, communication skills, and the ability to express ideas in front of others.

Random Acts of Kindness

Challenge yourself to perform random acts of kindness for strangers. It could be complimenting someone, helping with a task, or simply offering a friendly gesture. Stepping outside your comfort zone to connect with others builds empathy and social skills.

Start Talking with Someone New

Break the ice by starting a conversation with someone you don't know well. Whether it's a classmate, neighbor, or someone at a social event, taking the first step to connect with others helps broaden your social circle and improves communication skills.

Start a Passion Project

Identify a cause or interest that you're passionate about and start a project to contribute positively. This could be organizing a community event, launching a blog, or creating art with a purpose. Initiating and leading projects improves leadership skills and resilience.

☐ ☐ ☐ ☐ ☐

Volunteer in a New Environment

Step into a completely new volunteering environment. Choose a cause you're passionate about, and offer your time at a different organization or charity. This exposes you to different experiences and allows you to contribute to a broader community.

☐ ☐ ☐ ☐ ☐

Attend a Networking Event

Attend a networking event or career fair to practice introducing yourself, networking with professionals, and exploring potential career paths. This helps build confidence in social and professional settings.

☐ ☐ ☐ ☐ ☐

Try a New Physical Activity

Experiment with a physical activity you've never tried, such as rock climbing, surfing or martial arts. Physical challenges not only promote a healthy lifestyle but also boost confidence and self-esteem.

☐ ☐ ☐ ☐ ☐

Write about a Time You Overcame a Fear

Recall a moment when you faced a fear or stepped out of your comfort zone. Describe the experience, the emotions you felt, and how it impacted you. What did you learn about yourself in the process?

Imagine Your Dream Adventure

Close your eyes and imagine an adventurous scenario you've always dreamed of but never experienced. It could be a solo trip, trying a new sport, or learning a challenging skill. Describe the details of this dream adventure and how you envision yourself mastering it.

Letter to Future You

Write a letter to your future self, specifically focusing on the courageous decisions and new experiences you hope to have. Reflect on the growth you expect and encourage your future self to welcome opportunities outside of your comfort zone.

"People judge by outward appearance, but the Lord looks at the heart." – 1 Samuel 16:7

Boldly Me

Part 3

Cultivate Self-Worth

Boldly Me

Self-Worth

Think of self-worth as a strong, tall tree inside you. The roots of this tree are your **faith, positive thoughts**, and **personal values**. They keep you grounded and give you the courage to face the world.

Picture the tree trunk as your core – your strength and resilience. Self-worth means believing in your own value and knowing you're deserving of love, respect, and happiness. It's like your inner voice saying, "I'm perfect just the way I am."

Now, see the branches stretching out with leaves that represent your accomplishments, dreams, and what makes you uniquely you. Your self-worth grows in these leaves, celebrating your own specialness.

Building self-worth isn't about striving for perfection but rather about accepting and treating yourself kindly along your journey. It involves recognizing your strengths, acknowledging your worthiness of love and success, and understanding that your unique qualities contribute to the beauty of the world around you.

So let this tree of self-worth be a guiding force in your magnificent garden. Let's help it grow by saying kind words to ourselves, like watering it with positivity. Each time you achieve something, it's like a new leaf growing on your tree. And always remember, just like a tree grows taller and stronger, you are still growing into the amazing person you're meant to be, and your worthiness is already rooted within you.

Cultivate Self-Worth

List 10 or more different values, such as honesty, compassion, and creativity, that are important to you.

Take your identified values and rank them in order of importance.

1
2
3
4
5
6
7
8
9
10

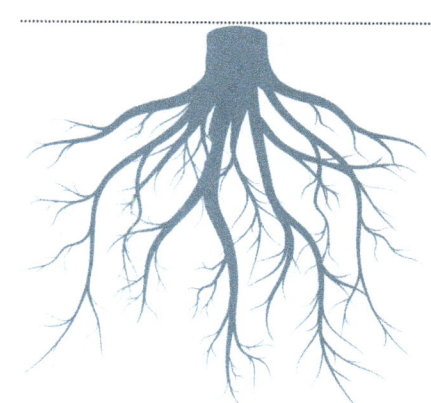

Building On Your Values

Values Reflection Journal

Get a journal just for exploring your values. Start by thinking about different parts of your life - family, friendships, school, hobbies, and more. Write about times when you felt really happy or proud. What were you doing, and what values were important in those moments?

Values Vision Board

Get creative with a visual representation of your values. Collect images, quotes, or symbols that represent what matters most to you. Arrange them in your journal as a visual reminder of your core values. Write short reflections about why each element aligns with your values.

Values in Action Challenge

Challenge yourself weekly or monthly to align your actions with a specific value. For instance, if kindness is important to you, challenge yourself to perform one act of kindness each day. Reflect in your journal on how these intentional actions contribute to your self-worth.

protea

Cultivate Self-Worth

Crafting Values Affirmations

Create affirmations based on your values. Write statements reinforcing your commitment to these values and declare them as truths about yourself. Make these affirmations part of your daily routine to boost self-worth and align your mindset with your values.

Regular Values Check-In

Regularly check in with your values. Take time each month or every few months to think about them in your journal. Think about whether your actions match up with what you believe in, and celebrate when they do. Use these reflections to make changes if needed and to remind yourself of your worth.

AFFIRMATION EXAMPLES

I treat others with compassion and understanding, knowing that kindness makes a difference.

I respect others' opinions, even when they differ from my own, growing understanding and open-mindedness.

I always strive to do the right thing, even when it's difficult, because integrity is at the core of who I am.

As you engage in these activities, you are not just exploring your values; you are actively shaping the way you navigate the world, making conscious choices that align with your true self.

Boldly Me

Cultivate Self-Worth

What Does The Bible Teaches About VALUES?

Love
"A new command I give you: Love one another. As I have loved you, so you must love one another."

John 13:34 (NIV)

Honesty/Integrity
"The Lord detests lying lips, but he delights in people who are trustworthy."

Proverbs 12:22 (NIV)

Compassion/Kindness
"Be kind and compassionate to one another, forgiving each other, just as in Christ God forgave you."

Ephesians 4:32 (NIV)

Humility
"Do nothing out of selfish ambition or vain conceit. Rather, in humility value others above yourselves."

Philippians 2:3 (NIV)

Generosity
"A generous person will prosper; whoever refreshes others will be refreshed."

Proverbs 11:25 (NIV)

Forgiveness
"Bear with each other and forgive one another if any of you has a grievance against someone. Forgive as the Lord forgave you."

Colossians 3:13 (NIV)

Gratitude
Give thanks in all circumstances; for this is God's will for you in Christ Jesus."

1 Thessalonians 5:18 (NIV)

Patience
"Be completely humble and gentle; be patient, bearing with one another in love."

Ephesians 4:2 (NIV)

Boldly Me

Cultivate Self-Worth

Bible VALUE Cards

Courage
"Have I not commanded you? Be strong and courageous. Do not be afraid; do not be discouraged, for the Lord your God will be with you wherever you go."

Joshua 1:9 (NIV)

Faithfulness
"Let love and faithfulness never leave you; bind them around your neck, write them on the tablet of your heart."

Proverbs 3:3 (NIV)

Self-Control
"But the fruit of the Spirit is love, joy, peace, forbearance, kindness, goodness, faithfulness, gentleness and self-control."

Galatians 5:22-23 (NIV)

Wisdom
"The fear of the Lord is the beginning of wisdom, and knowledge of the Holy One is understanding."

Proverbs 9:10 (NIV

Responsibility
"Each of you should use whatever gift you have received to serve others, as faithful stewards of God's grace in its various forms."

1 Peter 4:10 (NIV)

Friendship
"A friend loves at all times, and a brother is born for a time of adversity."

Proverbs 17:17 (NIV)

Respect
"Show proper respect to everyone, love the family of believers, fear God, honor the emperor."

1 Peter 2:17 (NIV)

Joy
"May the God of hope fill you with all joy and peace as you trust in him, so that you may overflow with hope by the power of the Holy Spirit."

Romans 15:13 (NIV)

Boldly Me

Cultivate Self-Worth

Mindfulness & Gratitude

On the journey to embracing your bold and beautiful self, mindfulness and gratitude join forces as empowering companions. Mindfulness, which is about being fully present without judgment, helps you understand yourself better and nurtures a positive sense of self-worth.

With mindfulness, you can observe your thoughts and feelings without being too hard on yourself. This practice frees you from negative self-perceptions and helps you see your inherent value. Instead of dwelling on mistakes or worrying about the future, mindfulness encourages you to focus on your strengths in the here and now, recognizing your worthiness.

When paired with gratitude, mindfulness becomes a superpower to escape the comparison trap. Grounded in the present, you let go of the pressure to measure your worth against others. You start celebrating your unique qualities and contributions, appreciating what makes you distinctly you.

This combination empowers you to appreciate your strengths, acknowledge your intrinsic value, and face life with a bold sense of acceptance. Embrace your boldly unique self, for you are worthy, and your journey is uniquely yours.

Boldly Me
Mindfulness Exercises

For the upcoming week, aim to practice one of these exercises daily. On the next page, write down how you feel and what your experience was.

Body Scan

- Find a quiet place to lie down or sit comfortably. Close your eyes and focus on each part of your body.
- Acknowledge any tension and focus on releasing that tension. Start with your scalp and end with your toes.

Mindful Breathing

- Practice deep, intentional breathing.
- Inhale slowly, hold for a moment and exhale gradually. Focus on the sensation of your breath to bring awareness to the present moment.

Visualization

- Imagine a place where you feel completely at peace and happy.
- Visualize yourself in this beautiful environment, accepting positive feelings about who you are.

Compassionate Self-Talk

- Notice any negative self-talk and replace it with compassionate and supportive phrases.
- Speak to yourself as you would to a good friend, offering encouragement and understanding.

Cultivate Self-Worth

Body Scan

- Find a quiet place to lie down or sit comfortably. Close your eyes and focus on each part of your body.
- Acknowledge any tension and focus on releasing that tension. Start with your scalp and end with your toes.

Body Scan

....

....

....

....

....

....

....

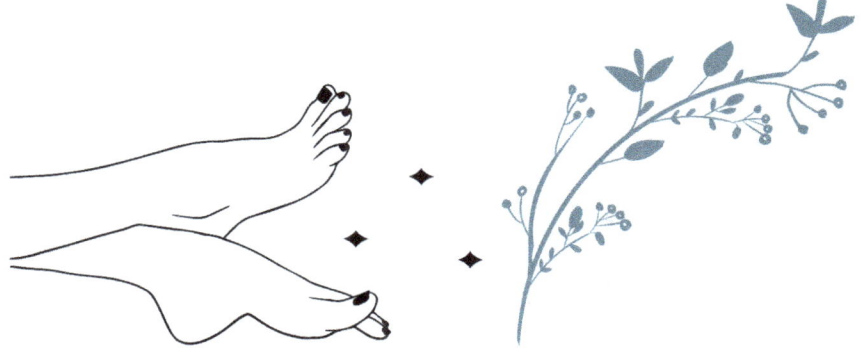

Mindful Breathing

- Practice deep, intentional breathing.
- Inhale slowly, hold for a moment and exhale gradually. Focus on the sensation of your breath to bring awareness to the present moment.

Mindful Breathing

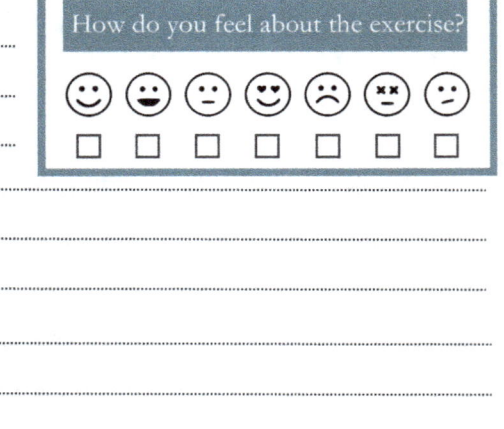

Cultivate Self-Worth

Compassionate Self-Talk

- Notice any negative self-talk and replace it with compassionate and supportive phrases.
- Speak to yourself as you would to a good friend, offering encouragement and understanding.

Compassionate Self-Talk

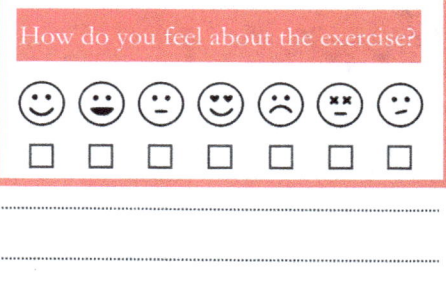

How do you feel about the exercise?

Visualization Exercise

- Imagine a place where you feel completely at peace and content.
- Visualize yourself in this beautiful environment, accepting positive feelings about who you are.

Visualization Exercise

Cultivate Self-Worth

Help Nina find the flowers

Puzzle 2

More Mindfulness Exercises

Five Senses Check-In

- Engage your five senses to anchor yourself in the present.
- Identify five things you can see, four things you can touch, three things you can hear, two things you can smell, and one thing you can taste.

Nature Walks

- Take a leisurely walk in nature.
- Pay attention to the sights, sounds, and smells around you.
- Connect with the beauty of the outdoors to nurtures a sense of presence.

Mindful Eating

- Practice mindful eating by savoring each bite without distractions.
- Pay attention to the flavors, textures, and smells of your food.

Creative Expression

- Engage in creative activities such as drawing, painting, or writing.
- Expressing yourself creatively helps you stay present and in touch with your emotions.

Mindful Listening

- Practice active listening during conversations.
- Focus on what the other person is saying without formulating your response in your mind. This promotes deeper connections.

Cultivate Self-Worth

Let's Practice Gratitude

Today, I am grateful for...

Think of three specific things that happened today for which you are grateful.

....
....
....
....
....

Someone who made me smile...

Write about someone who brought joy to your day and why their presence or actions made you smile.

....
....
....
....
....

Things I love about myself...

List three qualities or aspects about yourself that you appreciate and love.

....
....
....
....
....

Nature's beauty...
Write about something beautiful in nature that caught your attention or brought a feeling of peace.

Acts of kindness...
Note down any acts of kindness you witnessed or experienced today, no matter how small.

God's Faithfulness...
Reflect on a specific moment in your life where you experienced God's faithfulness. Write about how His presence and guidance impacted the situation and express your gratitude for His unwavering love.

Cultivate Self-Worth

Blessings in Disguise ...

Think about a challenging situation you faced that turned out to be a blessing in disguise. Write about how God worked through the difficulties, revealing His purpose and providing unexpected blessings. Express gratitude for His power and wisdom.

Answered Prayers ...

Write about specific instances where you witnessed God answering your prayers, either in the way you expected or in a way that surprised you. Write a letter to God expressing your gratitude for His attentive ear and His perfect timing in responding to your needs.

Boldly Me

Self-Care

In the whirlwind of teenage life, it's crucial to carve out moments just for you, moments that nourish your spirit, fuel your energy, and bring a sparkle to your soul.

1 Embrace the Morning Glow

Start your day with a burst of positivity. Greet the morning with a smile, stretch your limbs, and take a moment to appreciate the sunrise. Whether it's a few minutes of gentle stretching, deep breathing, or a favorite song, begin your mornings with the magic of self-love.

2 Digital Detox

Consider a digital detox to reclaim your morning. Put your phone on silent, resist the urge to check messages immediately, and relish the freedom of being present in the quiet morning hours. Connect with your faith, read a passage from your Bible, and spend a few moments in prayer.

3 Create Your Sanctuary

Designate a space in your room as your sanctuary. Fill it with things that bring you joy – comfy pillows, inspiring quotes, or twinkling fairy lights. This is your retreat, a place to unwind, reflect, and be entirely yourself.

Cultivate Self-Worth

4 Mindful Moments

In the hustle of the day, gift yourself mindful breaks. Whether it's enjoying a warm cup of tea, taking a nature walk, or simply pausing to breathe, these moments are a reset button for your mind and spirit.

5 Pamper Your Body

Your body is a treasure, so treat it with kindness. Whether it's a refreshing morning shower, a skincare routine, or a healthy breakfast, pamper yourself. It's not just about the physical care; it's about looking after your body that carries your vibrant spirit.

6 Unleash Creativity

Embrace your artistic side. Whether it's doodling in a sketchbook, expressing emotions through writing, or trying out a new craft, let your creativity flow. It's a beautiful way to connect with your inner self and discover hidden talents.

7 Reading and Quiet Time

Before you go to bed, spend some quiet time with your Bible. Pick a part that feels important to you, think about what it means, and spend a few moments talking to God. This special time with your faith can help you feel calm and understand things better before you go to sleep.

8 Restful Sleep Rituals

Create a soothing bedtime routine. Turn down the lights, do something relaxing, and snuggle up in a comfy spot. Good sleep is something magical that makes you feel refreshed and strong.

This serves as a model for a morning routine. Turn to the next page to craft your personalized daily routine. Feel free to duplicate that page and integrate it into your daily life.

Morning Routine

✓ **Wake up early**

✓ **Read my Bible and pray**

✓ **Drink a glass of water**

✓ **Wash my face**

✓ **Stretch / Exercise**

✓ **Eat a healthy breakfast**

✓ **Make my bed**

✓ **Take a shower**

✓ **Organize my day**

✓ **Set my daily goals / affirmations**

✓ **Ready for the day**

Cultivate Self-Worth

Self-Care Routine

DATE: _____ WEEK: _____

MORNING ROUTINE	M	T	W	T	F	S	S
	○	○	○	○	○	○	○
	○	○	○	○	○	○	○
	○	○	○	○	○	○	○
	○	○	○	○	○	○	○
	○	○	○	○	○	○	○
	○	○	○	○	○	○	○

EVENING ROUTINE	M	T	W	T	F	S	S
	○	○	○	○	○	○	○
	○	○	○	○	○	○	○
	○	○	○	○	○	○	○
	○	○	○	○	○	○	○
	○	○	○	○	○	○	○
	○	○	○	○	○	○	○

NOTES

Boldly Me

(Daily) SELF-CARE

DATE ___ / ___ / ___

S M T W T F S

CHECKLIST

- ○ make my bed
- ○ take my medications & vitamins
- ○ skincare routine
- ○ healthy meals
- ○ go for a walk
- ○ cleaning my room
- ○ washing clothes
- ○ listen to music
- ○ have a power nap
- ○ social media break

- ○ take a long bath
- ○ do a face mask
- ○ call a friend or family
- ○ pray / quiet time / meditation
- ○ watch a movie
- ○ cuddle a pet or human
- ○ try a new restaurant
- ○ make time to read
- ○ try a new food
- ○ no phone 30 mins before bed

WORKOUT
- ○ cardio   ○ pilates
- ○ stretch   ○ rest day
- ○ weight   ○ other

THINGS THAT MAKE ME HAPPY TODAY

HOURS OF SLEEP (Hours)

1 2 3 4 5 6 7 8

WATER BALANCE (Glass)

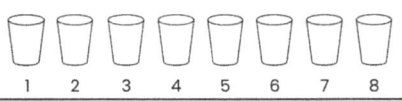

1 2 3 4 5 6 7 8

MOOD

ANGRY TIRED SAD GREAT FUN

Cultivate Self-Worth

Boldly Me

Part 4

Embrace Individuality

Understanding Uniqueness

Uniqueness means being different from everyone else. It's what makes you special and one-of-a-kind, including your personality, talents, interests, and experiences. Understanding what makes you unique is important when figuring out who you are – it's that remarkable thing that sets you apart from everyone else and makes you special.

You can also think of your uniqueness as a beautiful garden filled with various flowers, each representing a different aspect of who you are. There are flowers of laughter, tears, winning moments, and tough challenges.

It's a mix of your experiences, the things you love, your quirks, and your dreams, creating a one-of-a-kind landscape. This garden is always changing, always interesting.

As you look back on your life so far, think about all the different colors and varieties of flowers that make up your uniqueness—it's a beautiful garden just waiting for you to explore and celebrate.

Sometimes, it feels as if everyone wants you to be the same, to fit into a certain mold. But remember, your uniqueness is not a piece of a puzzle that has to match everyone else's – it's more like a truly fascinating garden full of exciting possibilities.

This section of the book is your guide, helping you unravel and understand all the amazing things that make you special. It's an invitation to enjoy the wonderful colors and fragrances that paint the picture of your life.

Remember that being unique isn't just about being different; it's about accepting, expressing, and falling in love with the wonderful, real you.

Embrace Individuality

Own Your Uniqueness

Diversity is Beautiful:

Just as you celebrate what makes you special, take a moment to appreciate the diversity around you. Every girl is a unique flower in the garden of life. Our differences make the world a more interesting and beautiful place.

Passions Make You Shine

What lights up your world? Whether it's playing an instrument, writing, sports, or a cause you deeply care about, your passions are like the stars in your sky. Develop them, let them shine, and watch how they make you glow from within.

Perfectly Imperfect

Newsflash: perfection is overrated! You're not meant to be flawless because it's the little quirks and imperfections that make you extraordinary. Embrace your uniqueness, and remember that it's okay not to have it all figured out.

Confidence is Your Superpower

The more you understand and love the fantastic person you are, the more confidence you'll gain. Confidence is like your superhero cape – wear it proudly. Stand tall, believe in yourself, and let the world see the incredible girl you are.

Celebrate Your Unseen Strengths

Consider the strengths and qualities within you that might not be immediately visible. It could be your ability to bounce-back, kindness, or ability to uplift others. Celebrate these unseen strengths that make you even more remarkable.

Explore Your Unique Style

Your style is an expression of your personality. Experiment with different clothing, accessories, or even hairstyles that reflect the real you. Your unique style is a powerful way to express your individuality.

Embrace Individuality

Show Your Uniqueness

Just like a garden blooms with many different kinds of flowers, each person adds something special to the world. To understand what makes you unique, there are three important steps to follow: acknowledge diversity by appreciating and celebrating the differences in others, learn to express yourself through activities like art, music, or writing, and share your creations proudly with the world. By doing this, you'll discover what makes you special and help make the world a more colorful and interesting place, so be proud of who you are and let your uniqueness shine!

1 Acknowledge Diversity

2 Express Yourself

3 Sharing Your Creations

1. Acknowledge Diversity

In a world with so many different people, seeing the beauty in our differences is important. Acknowledging diversity means recognizing and celebrating the unique qualities, backgrounds, and experiences that each person brings to the table. It's about understanding that everyone is different and that those differences should be respected and valued. By acknowledging diversity, we create an inclusive environment where everyone feels seen, heard, and appreciated for who they are.

List three things that make you different from your closest friend.

....

....

....

....

....

....

Take a moment to think about what makes your friends, family, and even strangers unique. What can you learn from their experiences and perspectives?

....

....

....

....

....

....

....

....

Embrace Individuality

Share a story about a time when someone's unique perspective helped you see things in a new light.

2. Express Yourself

Expressing yourself is like shining a light on the unique colors of your personality. When you share your thoughts, feelings, and talents with the world, you not only communicate who you are but also discover more about yourself in the process. It's through self-expression that you uncover what makes you truly unique.

Try out different creative activities like drawing, writing, or crafting. These aren't about being perfect; they're about letting your thoughts and feelings come to life.

Drawing

Pick a theme that excites you or represents something about yourself. Draw whatever comes to mind without worrying about perfection. It could be your favorite place, a dream you have, or simply doodles that express your emotions. Use the next page to do your first drawing.

Writing

Write about your day and your dreams, or even create short stories. Use this space to explore your thoughts without judgment. You can even start a journal where you can freely express yourself daily with these writing activities. Use the next page for your first writing activity.

Crafting

Get hands-on with crafting! Whether it's making a vision board, creating DIY projects, or experimenting with different materials, let your creativity flow. The goal is to enjoy the process and see where your imagination takes you.

Embrace Individuality

Drawing

Boldly Me

Writing

Embrace Individuality

Crafting

Write down / brainstorm what different crafting projects you are thinking of doing.

3. Sharing Your Creations

Once you've expressed yourself through your chosen activity, consider sharing it with others. This can be a powerful way to connect with people who might resonate with your experiences or appreciate your unique perspective.

Share your creations with friends or family and discuss what inspired you. Ask them about their own creative outlets and what they enjoy doing..

Consider sharing your creations on social media or creative platforms if you're comfortable. This can be a way to connect with a broader community and inspire others to express their uniqueness.

Reminder

Be aware that even though social media aims to bring together those who are alike, you might receive varied opinions, including negative feedback. Remember, it's perfectly fine – your uniqueness and passion might not be everyone's cup of tea, and that's what makes you extraordinary.

Favorite Quirks

Embrace your quirks! List three things about yourself that might be considered quirky or unconventional. Why do you love these unique aspects of yourself?

....
....
....
....
....
....
....

Style Statement

Your style is an expression of your personality. Describe your favorite outfit or accessory that reflects your individuality. How does it make you feel when you wear it?

....
....
....
....
....
....
....
....

Bucket List

What's something unusual or unique you want to do in your lifetime? Create a bucket list that includes activities or experiences that showcase your adventurous spirit.

Cultural Influences

Explore and celebrate your cultural background. Share a tradition, custom, or aspect of your cultural heritage that you cherish and feel proud of.

Inspiring Role Models

Identify a role model who embraces their individuality. What qualities do they possess that you admire, and how can you include those qualities in your own life?

Scrapbooking

Use the space below to showcase who you are. You can use drawings, magazine cutouts, words etc.

Boldly Me

Part 5

Social Connections

Boldly Me

Relationships

A healthy relationship is a connection between individuals characterized by mutual respect, open communication, trust, support, and a shared understanding of boundaries. It contributes to the well-being and personal growth of each person involved.

Here are some key components that define a healthy relationship:

Respect

In a healthy relationship, there is a deep and mutual respect for each other's opinions, values, and boundaries. Respect forms the foundation for trust and creates an environment where both individuals feel valued and appreciated.

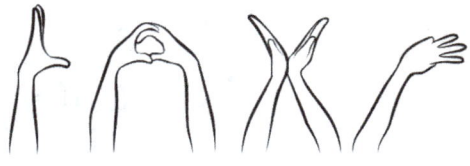

Communication

Effective communication is vital. Both parties should feel comfortable expressing their thoughts, feelings, and needs openly. This includes active listening, empathy, and a willingness to understand each other's perspectives.

Trust

Trust is built through consistency, reliability, and transparency. In a healthy relationship, both individuals have confidence in each other's honesty, reliability, and intentions. Trust forms the basis for emotional security.

Shared Values

While differences are natural and even celebrated, a healthy relationship often involves a foundation of shared values, goals, and priorities. This alignment helps create a sense of unity and common purpose.

Support

Healthy relationships provide emotional support during both good and challenging times. Friends encourage each other's goals and aspirations, offering comfort and assistance when needed. Support creates an environment where individuals can thrive and grow.

Adaptability

Life is dynamic, and a healthy relationship adapts to changes and challenges. Partners navigate life's ups and downs together, demonstrating resilience and a commitment to growth.

Positive Environment

A healthy relationship is characterized by positivity. Positive reinforcement, appreciation, and encouragement create an environment that nurtures happiness and contentment.

Independence

In a healthy relationship, each person maintains a sense of individuality. Both friends have their own interests, activities, and personal space. Independence is cherished and respected, promoting a balanced and fulfilling connection.

Conflict Resolution

Arguments might happen sometimes, but good friendships don't hold it against each other; instead, they find ways to solve problems in a positive way. Friends work together to find solutions, understanding that conflicts can be opportunities for growth and understanding.

Balance

Healthy relationships strike a balance between togetherness and independence. Both individuals have their own lives and interests while also enjoying shared activities and experiences.

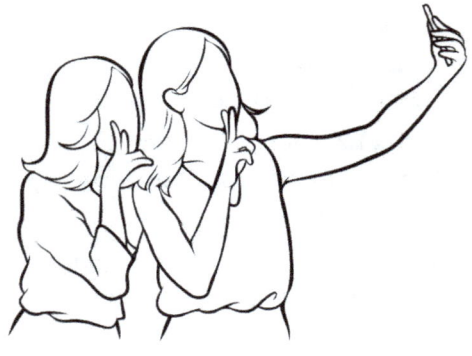

Social Connections

Setting Friendship Boundaries

Boundaries are like the protective walls surrounding our emotional and mental space, helping us define who we are and how we interact with the world. Establishing and understanding these limits isn't just about rules; it's a vital aspect of self-care and personal development.

This journey into boundary-setting becomes an empowering tool, creates healthy relationships, promotes self-respect, and ultimately contributes to your overall well-being as you navigate the complexities of adolescence.

Here's a list of common friendship boundaries that will help you to be a good friend :

Respecting Each Other's Time

Be aware of how often you chat or message each other. It's good to find a balance that works for both of you.

Giving Personal Space

Everyone needs some alone time. Respect your friend's personal space and don't pry into their private matters.

Understanding Time Commitments

We all have busy schedules. Make sure to consider your friend's schedule and be realistic about how much time you can spend together.

Respecting Feelings

Pay attention to how your friend feels, and treat their emotions with care. Avoid trying to make them feel guilty or manipulating them.

Being Reliable

If you make plans, try your best to stick to them. Let your friend know if something comes up or if you need to change the plans

Respecting Differences

People are different, and that's okay! Respect your friend's opinions and beliefs, even if they're not the same as yours.

Social Connections

Handling Conflicts

If you have a disagreement, talk about it calmly. Take a break if things get too intense, and come back to it when you both feel ready.

Sharing Belongings

Ask before borrowing something from your friend, and return it promptly in the same or better condition. Also, be clear about your own comfort level with lending things.

Offering Support

Ask your friend how you can support them. Don't assume — everyone needs different kinds of help.

Encouraging Independence

It's important to have your own interests and hobbies. Encourage your friend to pursue their passions, too.

Physical Contact

Respect your friend's comfort level with physical touch. Always ask before giving hugs or getting close.

Social Media Etiquette

Be mindful of your friend's privacy online. Avoid sharing personal details without permission.

Giving Feedback

If you have something to say, try to be constructive and kind. Listen when your friend gives feedback, too.

Balancing Socializing

Discuss how often you want to hang out as a group or one-on-one. It's okay to spend time on your own, too.

Remember, these are just guidelines, and it's essential to talk openly with your friend about what works best for both of you. Every friendship is unique, and finding a balance that suits both parties is the key to a healthy and happy relationship.

Social Connections

Reflect on how each friendship started. What drew you to each friend initially? What memories do you have from the beginning of your friendships?

....
....
....
....
....
....
....
....

Recall specific adventures or experiences you've shared with your friends. What made these moments memorable, and how have they strengthened your bond?

....
....
....
....
....
....
....
....

Boldly Me

Write about times your friends have been there for you during challenges. How did their support impact you, and what did you learn from those experiences?

....
....
....
....
....
....
....
....
....
....

Write on any inside jokes or moments of shared laughter. What makes these moments special, and how do they contribute to the joy in your friendships?

....
....
....
....
....
....
....
....
....

Social Connections

List the qualities in each friend that you admire the most. How do these qualities enhance your friendships and contribute to your personal growth?

....
....
....
....
....
....
....
....
....
....

Imagine future adventures and experiences you'd like to share with your friends. What are your hopes and aspirations for your friendships moving forward?

....
....
....
....
....
....
....
....
....
....

As we reach the final pages of Boldly Me, I want you to take a moment to reflect on your incredible journey of self-discovery and empowerment. This book was crafted with the belief that you are a unique masterpiece, a creation designed with purpose, love, and endless potential.

You Are Enough:
Remember, you are not defined by societal standards, comparison, or fleeting trends. You are fearfully and wonderfully made, and your journey towards self-love is a testament to the strength and beauty within you.

Celebrate Your Uniqueness:
Embrace your quirks, your dreams, and every facet of your being. "Boldly Me" is not just a title; it's a call to action. Stand tall in the truth that you are one-of-a-kind, a radiant expression of individuality.

Embrace Growth:
The journey to self-love and confidence is ongoing. Just as a flower continues to bloom, so do you. Embrace the growth, learning, and evolving process into the best version of yourself.

Impact Others Positively:
Your uniqueness is not just for personal fulfillment; it's a gift to share with the world. As you boldly embrace your true self, you inspire others to do the same. Your authenticity has the power to create ripples of positive change.

Stay Connected:
This book is not the end; it's a beginning. Stay connected with the principles and practices you've discovered within these pages. Continue to set intentions, explore your passions, and surround yourself with positivity.

You Are Loved:
In your boldest moments and in times of vulnerability, remember that you are loved. God's love is the foundation upon which you can build your self-worth, confidence, and acceptance.

Boldly Me

Boldly Me

Puzzle Solutions

Puzzle 1

Z	B	S	X	F	X	I	Z	K	E	B	V	C	C	H	J	Z	C
T	R	R	T	V	X	Q	D	I	F	M	Q	Q	C	Y	Q	A	K
Q	E	M	P	A	T	H	E	T	I	C	G	H	Z	J	X	B	Z
N	S	Z	I	P	W	X	T	H	W	P	G	R	S	L	U	O	A
U	I	F	E	A	R	L	E	S	S	J	T	A	X	Y	Q	N	C
X	L	I	N	S	P	I	R	A	T	I	O	N	A	L	R	U	O
K	I	U	H	M	T	E	M	P	O	W	E	R	E	D	C	D	N
Q	E	Z	X	V	O	K	I	T	U	S	X	C	F	Y	N	Y	F
S	N	U	S	Y	F	R	N	I	U	V	H	T	C	K	J	W	I
V	T	U	D	Y	D	M	E	I	A	H	V	E	D	Y	B	A	D
L	F	P	C	G	O	I	D	I	A	J	F	N	A	W	X	A	E
J	F	X	C	A	P	A	B	L	E	X	A	A	R	G	P	U	N
T	G	N	P	P	O	K	C	Z	P	V	A	C	T	L	Z	B	T
V	L	G	I	D	Q	Z	Q	D	L	E	M	I	M	Q	N	X	H
L	F	O	Q	H	H	N	Y	S	O	U	U	O	I	J	H	A	V
Y	Z	C	J	J	Z	F	D	Z	K	X	A	F	U	E	S	V	P	H
D	K	X	C	O	U	R	A	G	E	O	U	S	S	C	C	L	M
U	B	B	C	G	A	O	K	Q	F	J	U	D	M	D	C	T	O

RESILIENT EMPOWERED CONFIDENT
TENACIOUS FEARLESS DETERMINED
CAPABLE INSPIRATIONAL COURAGEOUS
EMPATHETIC

Puzzle 2

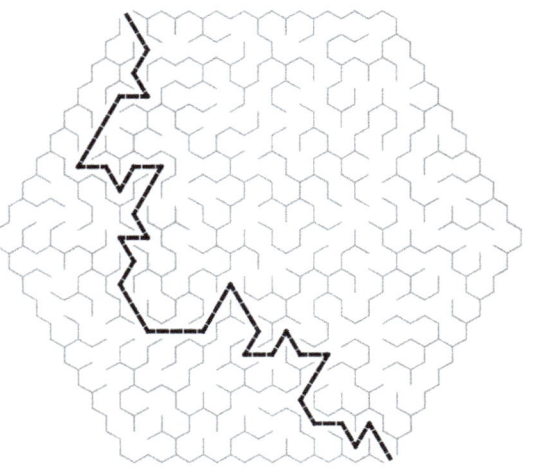

120

www.ingramcontent.com/pod-product-compliance
Lightning Source LLC
Chambersburg PA
CBHW070432010526
44118CB00014B/2005